April '80

To Ted & Renée
in friendship

Charles Brinds

CHARLES TOMLINSON

Written on Water

LONDON
OXFORD UNIVERSITY PRESS
1972

*Oxford University Press, Ely House, London W.*1

GLASGOW NEW YORK TORONTO MELBOURNE WELLINGTON
CAPE TOWN IBADAN NAIROBI DAR ES SALAAM LUSAKA ADDIS ABABA
DELHI BOMBAY CALCUTTA MADRAS KARACHI LAHORE DACCA
KUALA LUMPUR SINGAPORE HONG KONG TOKYO

ISBN 0 19 211820 X

© *Oxford University Press* 1972

PRINTED IN GREAT BRITAIN
BY THE BOWERING PRESS, PLYMOUTH

TO BRENDA

CONTENTS

IV. BAGATELLES

V. INSTEAD OF AN ENDING

ACKNOWLEDGEMENTS

Acknowledgements are due to the editors of the following periodicals in which some of these poems first appeared:
Agenda, The Critical Quarterly, The Hudson Review, Iowa Review, The Listener, London Magazine, The Michigan Quarterly, Organ (San Francisco), *Poetry Chicago, Stand, The Times Literary Supplement.*

NOTES

'Ariadne and the Minotaur' (p. 20) Suggested initially by Picasso's series of drawings, this ignores as they do the question of the actual kinship between Ariadne and the Minotaur. Perhaps she, too, was unaware of it.

'Machiavelli in Exile' (p. 21) *Tarde non furon mai grazie divine* (Divine graces were never late) is Machiavelli's misquotation of Petrarch's *Ma tarde non fur mai grazie divine.* It begins the letter to Francesco Vettori on which this poem is, in part, based.

'Over Elizabeth Bridge' (p. 43) László Rajk, Hungarian Foreign Minister, executed during the Stalinist period; Imre Nagy, Prime Minister and leader of the 1956 revolution, also executed. The poet, Attila József, killed himself in the thirties.

I. SEA PIECES

ON WATER

'FURROW' is inexact:
no ship could be
converted to a plough
travelling this vitreous ebony:

seal it in sea-caves and
you cannot still it:
image on image bends
where half-lights fill it

with illegible depths
and lucid passages,
bestiary of stones,
book without pages:

and yet it confers
as much as it denies:
we are orphaned and fathered
by such solid vacancies:

MACKINNON'S BOAT

FACED to the island, Mackinnon's boat
   Arcs out: the floats of his creels
Cling to the shelter half a mile away
   Of Tarner's cliff. Black, today
The waters will have nothing to do with the shaping
   Or unshaping of human things. No image
Twists beside the riding launch, there to repeat
   Its white and blue, its unrigged mast
Slanting from the prow in which a dog
   Now lies stretched out—asleep
It seems, but holds in steady view
   Through all-but-closed eyes the grey-black
Water travelling towards it. The surface,
   Opaque as cliffstone, moves scarred

3

By a breeze that strikes against its grain
  In ruffled hatchings. Distance has disappeared,
Washed out by mist, but a cold light
  Keeps here and there re-touching it,
Promising transparencies of green and blue
  Only to deny them. The visible sea
Remains a sullen frontier to
  Its unimaginable fathoms. The dog eyes
Its gliding shapes, but the signs he can recognize
  Are land signs: he is here
Because men are here, unmindful
  Of this underworld of Mackinnon's daily dealings.
As the creels come in, he'll lie
  Still watching the waters, nostrils
Working on seasmells, but indifferent
  To the emerging haul, clawed and crawling.
The cliff lifts near, and a guttural cry
  Of cormorants raises his glance: he stays
Curled round on himself: his world
  Ignores this waste of the in-between,
Air and rock, stained, crag-sheer
  Where cormorants fret and flock
Strutting the ledges. The two men
  Have sited their destination. Mackinnon
Steering, cuts back the engine and Macaskill
  Has the light floats firm and then
The weight of the freighted creels is on his rope—
  A dozen of them—the coil spitting
Water as it slaps and turns on the windlass
  Burning Macaskill's palms paying it in.
As the cold, wet line is hauled, the creels
  Begin to arrive. And, inside, the flailing
Seashapes pincered to the baits, drop
  Slithering and shaken off like thieves
Surprised, their breath all at once grown rare
  In an atmosphere they had not known existed.
Hands that have much to do yet, dealing
  With creel on creel, drag out the catch
And feeling the cage-nets, re-thread each fault.
  Crabs, urchins, dogfish, and star,
All are unwanted and all are
  Snatched, slaughtered, or flung to their freedom—
Some, shattering on the cordage

They too eagerly clung to. Hands must be cruel
To keep the pace spry to undo and then
    To re-tie, return the new-baited traps
To water, but an ease makes one
    The disparate links of the concerted action
Between the first drawing in
    And the let down crash of stone-weighted baskets.
There is more to be done still. The trough of the gunwhale
    Is filled with the scrabbling armour of defeat;
Claw against claw, not knowing
    What it is they fight, they swivel
And bite on air until they feel
    The palpable hard fingers of their real
Adversary close on them; and held
    In a knee-grip, must yield to him.
The beaked claws are shut and bound
    By Mackinnon. Leaning against the tiller,
He impounds each one alive
    In the crawling hatch. And so the boat
Thrusts on, to go through a hundred and more creels
    Before the return. Macaskill throws
To Mackinnon a cigarette down the length
    Of half the craft. Cupping,
They light up. Their anonymity, for a spell,
    Is at an end, and each one
Free to be himself once more
    Sharing the rest that comes of labour.
But labour must come of rest: and already
    They are set towards it, and soon the floats
Of the next creel-drift will rise
    Low in the water. An evasive light
Brightens like mist rolling along the sea,
    And the blue it beckoned—blue
Such as catches and dies in an eye-glance—
    Glints out its seconds. Making a time
Where no day has a name, the smells
    Of diesel, salt, and tobacco mingle:
They linger down a wake whose further lines
    Are beginning to slacken and fall back to where
Salt at last must outsavour name and time
    In the alternation of the forgetful waters.

                                        Ullinish

5

THE THIEF'S JOURNAL

Only this book of love will be real. What of the facts which served as its pretext? I must be their repository.—Genet

How much there was had escaped him:
The suns were outpacing his vagrancy:
He had crossed Andalusia. Andalusia
Was what it was still to be
Without him. It tantalized imagination
The taste of the fish he had eaten there without salt or bread
At his sea-wrack fire whose ashes
The careful sea had long-since appropriated.

ROWER

A PLOTLESS tale: the passing hours
    Bring in a day that's nebulous. Glazes of moist pearl
Mute back the full blaze of a sea,
    Drifting continually where a slack tide
Has released the waters. Shallows
    Spread their transparency, letting through
A pale-brown map of sandbanks
    Barely submerged, where a gull might wade
Thin legs still visible above its blurred reflection.
    It seems nothing will occur here until
The tide returns, ferrying to the shore it freshness,
    Beating and breaking only to remake itself
The instant the advancing line goes under.
    And nothing does. Except for the inching transformations
Of a forenoon all melting redundancies
    Just beyond eyeshot: the grey veils
Drink-in a little more hidden sunlight,
    Shadows harden, pale. But then
Out into the bay, towards deeper water,
    Sidles the rower, gaining speed
As he reaches it. Already his world
    Is sliding by him. Backwards
He enters it, eyes searching the past

6

Before them: that shape that crowns the cliff,
A sole, white plane, draws tight his gaze—
A house, bereft so it seems of time
By its place of vantage, high
    Over cleft and crack. When, as momentarily,
He steals a glance from it to fling
    Across his travelling shoulder, his eyes
Soon settle once more along that line
    Tilted towards the shoremark. And though the ripple
Is beneath him now—the pull and beat
    Unfelt when further in—he cuts athwart it
Making his way, to the liquid counterpulse
    Of blades that draw him outwards to complete
The bay's half-circle with his own. Muscle
    And bone work to that consummation of the will
Where satisfaction gathers to surfeit, strain
    To ease. Pleased by his exertions, he abandons them
Riding against rested oars, subdued
    For the moment to that want of purpose
In sky and water, before he shoots
    Feathering once more baywards, his face
To the direction the tide will take when
    Out of the coherent chaos of a morning that refuses
To declare itself, it comes plunging in
    Expunging the track of his geometries.

THE LIGHTHOUSE

THE lighthouse is like the church of some island sect
    Who have known the mainland beliefs and have defected
Only to retain them in native purity
    And in the daily jubilation of storm and sea,
But adding every day new images
    To their liturgy of changes—each one
Some myth over and done with now
    Because sea has rebegotten land and land
The sea, and all is waiting to declare
    That things have never been praised for what they were,
        emerging
Along promontory on enfiladed promontory.

I. LE RENDEZ-VOUS DES PAYSAGES

THE promenade, the plage, the paysage
all met somewhere
in the reflection of a reflection
in midair: cars, unheard,
were running on water: jetplanes
lay on their backs
like sunbathers
in a submarine graveyard
about to resurrect into the fronds
of ghost-palms boasting
'We exist'
to the sea's uncertain mirrors
to the reversed clocktowers that had lost
all feeling for time
suspended
among the overlapping vistas
of promenade, plage, paysage.

II. LA PROMENADE DE PROTÉE

CHANGING, he walks the changing avenue:
this blue and purple are the blue
and purple of autumn underwater:
they are changing to green and he
is changing to an undulated statue
in this sea-floor park
and does not know
if the iced green will undo him
or which are real
among the recollections that cling
to him and seem to know him:
and hears overhead the shudder of departing keels.

STONE SPEECH

CROWDING this beach
are milkstones, white
teardrops; flints
edged out of flinthood
into smoothness chafe
against grainy ovals,
pitted pieces, nosestones,
stoppers and saddles;
veins of orange
inlay black beads:
chalk-swaddled babyshapes,
tiny fists, facestones
and facestone's brother
skullstone, roundheads
pierced by a single eye,
purple finds, all
rubbing shoulders:
a mob of grindings,
groundlings, scatterings
from a million necklaces
mined under sea-hills, the pebbles
are as various as the people.

THE SEA IS OPEN TO THE LIGHT

THE sea is open to the light:
the image idling
beneath the skerry
is the unmoving
skerry's own
rockbound foundation
travelling down and down
to meet in the underdeeps
the spread floor
shadowed where the fish
flash in their multitude
transmitting and eluding
the illumination.

VARIATION ON PAZ

Hay que . . . soñar hacia dentro y tambien hacia afuera

WE must dream inwards, and we must dream
   Outwards too, until—the dream's ground
Bound no longer by the dream—we feel
   Behind us the sea's force, and the blind
Keel strikes gravel, grinding
   Towards a beach where, eye by eye,
The incorruptible stones are our witnessess
   And we wake to what is dream and what is real
Judged by the sun and the impartial sky.

II. BY THE MIDDLE SEA

THE COMPACT: AT VOLTERRA

THE crack in the stone, the black filament
    Reaching into the rockface unmasks
More history than Etruria or Rome
    Bequeathed this place. The ramparted town
Has long outlived all that; for what
    Are Caesar or Scipio beside
The incursion of the slow abyss, the daily
    Tribute the dry fields provide

Trickling down? There is a compact
    To undo the spot, between the unhurried sun
Edging beyond this scene, and the moon,
    Risen already, that has stained
Through with its pallor the remaining light:
    Unreal, that clarity of lips and wrinkles
Where shadow investigates each fold,
    Scaling the cliff to the silhouetted stronghold.

Civic and close-packed, the streets
    Cannot ignore this tale of unshorable earth
At the town brink; furrow, gully,
    And sandslide guide down
Each seeping rivulet only to deepen
    The cavities of thirst, dry out
The cenozoic skeleton, appearing, powdering away,
    Uncovering the chapped clay beneath it.

There is a compact between the cooling earth
    And every labyrinthine fault that mines it—
The thousand mouths whose language
    Is siftings, whisperings, rumours of downfall
That might, in a momentary unison,
    Silence all, tearing the roots of sound out
With a single roar: but the cicadas
    Chafe on, grapevine entwines the pergola

Gripping beyond itself. A sole farm
    Eyes space emptily. Those
Who abandoned it still wire
    Their vines between lopped willows:

Their terraces, fondling the soil together,
   Till up to the drop that which they stand to lose:
Refusing to give ground before they must,
   They pit their patience against the dust's vacuity.

The crack in the stone, the black filament
   Rooting itself in dreams, all live
At a truce, refuted, terracing; as if
   Unreasoned care were its own and our
Sufficient reason, to repair the night's derisions,
   Repay the day's delight, here where the pebbles
Of half-ripe grapes abide their season,
   Their fostering leaves outlined by unminding sky.

TWO POEMS OF LUCIO PICCOLO

I. UNSTILL UNIVERSE

UNSTILL universe of gusts
of rays, of hours without colour, of perennial
transits, vain displays
of cloud: an instant and—
look, the changed forms
blaze out, milennia grow unstable.
And the arch of the low door and the step
worn by too many winters, are a fable
in the unforeseen burst from the March sun.

II. VENERIS VENEFICA AGRESTIS

SHE springs from the ground-clinging thicket, her face
—gay now, now surly—bound in a black
kerchief, a shrivelled chestnut it seems: no fine fleece
the hair that falls loose, but a lock
of curling goat-hair; when she goes by

(is she standing or bending?) her gnarled and dark
foot is a root that suddenly juts from the earth and walks.
　　Be watchful she does not offer you her cup of bark,
its water root-flavoured that tastes of the viscid leaf,
either mulberry or sorb-apple, woodland fruit that flatters with
　　　　lies
the lips but the tongue ties.
　　She governs it seems
the force of rounding moons
that swells out the rinds of trees
and alternates the invincible ferments,
flow of the sap and of the seas. . . .
　　Pronubial, she, like the birds that bring
seeds from afar: arcane
the breeds that come of her grafting.
　　And the mud walls of the unstable
cottage where the nettle grows
with gigantic stalk, are her realms of shadows:
she ignites the kindlings in the furnaces of fable.
　　And round the door, from neighbouring orchard ground
the fumes that rise
are the fine, unwinding muslins of her sibiline vespers.
　　She appears in the guise
of the centipede among the darknesses
by water-wheels that turn
no more in the maidenhair fern.
　　She is the mask that beckons
and disappears, when the light
of the halfspent wicks
makes voracious the shadows in the room where
they are milling by night, working at the presses,
and odours of crushed olives are in the air,
kindled vapours of grapejuice; and lanterns come
swayed to the steps of hobnailed boots.
　　The gestures of those who labour
in the fields, are accomplices
in the plots she weaves:
the stoop of those who gather up dry leaves
and acorns . . . and the shoeless tread and measured bearing
under burdened head, when you cannot see
the brow or the olives of the eyes
but only the lively mouth . . . the dress
swathes tight the flanks, the breasts, and has comeliness—

passing the bough she leaves behind
an odour of parching . . .
or the gesture that raises the crock
renewed at the basin of the spring.
    She bends, drawing a circle:
her sign sends forth
the primordial torrent out of the fearful earth
(and the foot that presses the irrigated furrow
and the hand that lifts
the spade—power of a different desire summons them now);
she draws strength
from the breaths of the enclosures,
the diffused cries, the damp and burning
straw of the litters, the blackened
branches of the vine, and the shadow that gives back
the smell of harnesses of rope and sack,
damp baskets, where who stands
on the threshold can descry
the stilled millstone, hoes long used to the grip of rural hands:
the rustic shade ferments with ancestral longings.
    Rockroses, thistles, pulicaria, calaminths—scents
that seem fresh and aromatic, are
(should your wariness pall) the lures
of a spiral that winds-in all,
(night bites into silver
free of all alloy of sidereal ray) she will
blur in a fume of dust the gentle hill-curve.
    Now, she's in daylight, one hand against an oak,
the other hangs loose—filthy and coaxing,
her dress black as a flue-brush . . .
and the sudden rush of wind
over the headland, sets at large, lets flow
in a flood a divine
tangle of leaves and flourishing bough.
    The heat, too, promises, discloses
freshness, vigour of the breath that frees
peach and the bitter-sweet
odour of the flowering almond tree; under coarse leaf
are fleshy and violent mouths, wild offshoots,
between the ferns' long fans
obscure hints of mushroom growths,
uncertain glances of water glint through the clovers,
and a sense of bare

original clay is there
near where the poplar wakes unslakeable thirst
with its rustling mirages of streams
and makes itself a mirror of each breeze,
where, in the hill's shade,
steep sloping,
the valley grows
narrow and closes
in the mouth of a spring
among delicate mosses.
    If, for a moment,
cloud comes to rest
over the hill-crest or the valley threshold,
in the living shade
the shaft of that plough now shows
which shakes which unflowers unleafs
the bush and the forest rose.

AT SANT' ANTIMO

FLANKING the place,
a cypress
stretches itself, its surface
working as the wind
travels it in a continual
breathing, an underwater
floating of foliage
upwards, till
compact and wavering
it flexes a sinuous
tip that chases
its own shadow
to and fro
across the still
stone tower.

TARQUINIA

Vince Viet Cong! The testimony of walls.
What do they mean—'is winning'
Or 'let win'? In the beginning Tarquinia
Lorded ten provinces and has come to this,
A museum of tombstones, a necropolis.
Walls built of walls, the run-down
Etruscan capital is a town
Of bars and butchers' shops
Inside the wreck of palaces.
The Tomb of the Warriors. They are painted there
Carousing, drinking to victory. Said Forster,
'Let yourself be crushed.' They fought and were.
A woman goes past, bent by the weight
Of the trussed fowl she is trailing. The cross
Swings from her neck in accompaniment.
The eyes of the winged horses
That rode on the citadel are still keen
With the intelligence of a lost art.
Vince Viet Cong! What is it they mean?

SANTA MARIA DELLE NEVI

SANTA Maria
stands open
to the heat, a cave
of votive flames
that lure the eye
into the gloom
surrounding them. Lost
at first, one looks
for the ground and closure
to that fresh recess,
shallowly tunnelled-out
between its walls
and, in the end,

18

grasps it is the white
of painted snow
irradiates the altar-piece:
from bowl and salver
it overflows,
in snowballs like fruit,
an offering to
the Madonna of the Snows
and to the child
whom her restraining hands
hold steady,
its fingers curious
at the inexplicable
intimation of the cold:
an August dream,
and so exactly
does it fit the day
it seems to tally
with its opposite
in strength of fact,
where Santa Maria
hoards up the glow
of winter recollected
and summer inlays the street
as bright as snow.

THE SQUARE

A CONSOLIDATION
of voices in the street
below, a wave
that never reaches
its destination: the higher
voices of children
ride it and the raucous
monomaniac bikes
hunting their shadows
into the sunlight of the square

to a drum-roll
of metal shutters
sliding: and above it all
the reflection
hung on the open
pane (it opens
inwards)of the bell
over Santa Maria delle Nevi,
not even slightly
swung in the hot
evening air.

ARIADNE AND THE MINOTAUR

WHEN Theseus went down
she stood alone surrounded
by the sense of what finality it was
she entered now: the hot rocks offered her
neither resistance nor escape, but ran
viscous with the image of betrayal:
the pitted and unimaginable face
the minotaur haunted her with
kept forming there
along the seams and discolorations
and in the diamond sweat
of mica: the sword and thread
had been hers to give, and she
had given them, to this easer of destinies:
if she had gone
alone out of the sun and down where he
had threaded the way for her,
if she had gone
winding the ammonite of space
to where at the cold heart
from the dark stone the bestial warmth
would rise to meet her
unarmed in acquiescence, unprepared
her spindle of packthread . . . her fingers felt now

for the image in the sunlit rock, and her ears
at the shock of touch took up a cry
out of the labyrinth
into their own, a groaning
that filled the stone mouth
hollowly: between the lips of stone
appeared he whom she had sent
to go where her unspeakable
intent unspoken had been to go
herself, and heaved unlabyrinthed at her feet
their mutual completed crime—
a put-by destiny, a dying
look that sought her
out of eyes the light extinguished,
eyes she should have led
herself to light: and the rays
that turned to emptiness in them
filling the whole of space with loss,
a waste of irrefutable sunlight spread
from Crete to Naxos.

MACHIAVELLI IN EXILE

A MAN is watching down the sun. All day,
Exploring the stone sinew of the hills,
For his every predilection it has asked
A Roman reason of him. And he has tried
To give one, tied to a dwindling patrimony
And the pain of exile. His guileless guile,
Trusted by nobody, he is self-betrayed.

And yet, for all that, Borgia shall be praised
Who moved and, moving, saved by sudden action:
The Florentines, despite their words, will have
Faction and the blood that comes of faction:
The work of France and Spain others begin—
Let him who says so exercise his powers
With dice and backgammon at a country inn;

Where, for his day's companions, he must choose
Such men as endure history and not those
Who make it: with their shadows, magnified
And spread behind them, butcher, publican,
Miller, and baker quarrel at their cards,
And heights and hill-roads all around are filled
With voices of gods who do not know they're gods.

Nor are they, save for a trick of light and sound:
Their fate is bound by their own sleeping wills.
Though lateness shadows all that's left to do,
Tarde non furon mai grazie divine :
The sun that lit his mind now lights the page
At which he reads and words, hard-won, assuage
What chance and character have brought him to.

He enters that courtly ancient company
Of men whose reasons may be asked, and he,
Released from tedium, poverty, and threat,
Lives in the light of possibility:
Their words are warm with it, yet tempered by
The memory of its opposite, else too soon
Hopes are a mob that wrangle for the moon.

Adversity puts his own pen in hand,
First torture, then neglect bringing to bear
The style and vigilance which may perfect
A prince, that he whom history forsook
Should for no random principle forsake
Its truth's contingency, his last defeat
And victory, no battle, but a book.

III. OF LIGHT AND AIR

HAWKS

Hawks hovering, calling to each other
   Across the air, seem swung
Too high on the risen wind
   For the earth-clung contact of our world:
And yet we share with them that sense
   The season is bringing in, of all
The lengthening light is promising to exact
   From the obduracy of March. The pair,
After their kind are lovers and their cries
   Such as lovers alone exchange, and we
Though we cannot tell what it is they say,
   Caught up into their calling, are in their sway,
And ride where we cannot climb the steep
   And altering air, breathing the sweetness
Of our own excess, till we are kinned
   By space we never thought to enter
On capable wings to such reaches of desire.

OF BEGINNING LIGHT

The light of the mind is poorer
than beginning light: the shades
we find pigment for
poor beside the tacit
variety we can all see
yet cannot say: of beginning light
I will say this, that it dispenses
imperial equality to everything
it touches, so that purple
becomes common wear, but purple
resolving in its chord
a thousand tones
tinged by a thousand
shadows, all
yielding themselves
slowly up: and the mind,

feeling its way among
such hesitant distinctions,
is left behind as they
flare into certainties that
begin by ending them
in the light of day.

CARSCAPE

MIRRORED
the rear window
holds a glowing
almost-gone-day
scene, although the day
across this upland
has far to go: one drives
against its glare
that by degrees a moving
Everest of cloud
will shadow-over
while amid these
many vanishings
replenished, the wintry
autumnal afternoon
could still be dawn.

DRIVE

FIRST light strikes
across a landmass
daylight hides: horizon
rides above horizon
momentarily
like a region of cloud:
I return driving
to the same view undone:
the windscreen takes it in
as a high and brilliant
emptiness that lies to one
of no depth, stretched above
palpabilities morning could touch:
and one feels for the features of the lost
continent (it seems)
of day's beginnings, recollection
seizing on the mind
with what infinity of unmarked
mornings, of spaces unsounded
habit abjures, in the cross-
tides of chaos, till we
believe our eyes (our lies)
that there is nothing there
but what we see—
and drive

LEGEND

MIDAS eyes the seasonable glints:
    Pennywise, he hears the cash-crop
Clashing its foliage under the wind,
    As the buzz-saw in his mind
Bores through the pastoral irrelevance:
    Seen from this vantage, every view
Becomes a collector's item, and the atmosphere
    Squares off each parcel of bright worth
In bounding it: limbs to matchwood,
    Skyline saw-toothed to raw angles
Roof on roof, as Midas
    Stares the future into being, melts down
Season into season, past distinction,
    While the leaves too slowly
Deal their lightness to the air that lifts
    Then releases them on suppled boughs,
Time present beyond all bargain, liquid gifts.

AUTUMN PIECE

BAFFLED
by the choreography of the season
the eye could not
with certainty see
whether it was wind
stripping the leaves or
the leaves were struggling to be free:

They came at you
in decaying spirals
plucked flung and regathered by the same
force that was twisting
the scarves of the vapour trails
dragging all certainties out of course:

As the car resisted it
you felt it in either hand
commanding car, tree, sky,
master of chances,
and at a curve was a red
board said 'Danger':
I thought it said dancer.

THE WHITE VAN

new coated
a winter white
rides on ahead
through the brightness of
late autumn weather,
as the low and rising
side sun
flings from hedgerow
and from sky on to
its moving screen
a shadow show:
trees, half-unleafed,
fretted and pierced now
by sudden skylights,
come dancing down,
angle and mass and bough,
birds drawing them together
in their reflected flight:
this is all shape
and surface, you might say,
this black and white
abstraction of a coloured
day, but here
is no form so far
from what we see
it does not take the glow
and urgency of all
those goings-on

29

surrounding us: chance
unblinds certitude
with a fourth eye (the third
one is the mind's),
the paint of autumn
showing the more intense
for these pied
anatomies and
as the white van turns
right, distance
ahead of us
re-opens its density
of gold, green, amethyst.

IN OCTOBER

A WEATHER of flashes, fragments
of Pentecost restored
and lost before the tongue
has time for them. The word
is brought to nothing
that caught at burning bushes
gone already and at vistas
where there are none. For now
it must speak of the wreck
two rainbows make that
half-expunged, hang
broken above each other
footlessly balancing.

URLICHT

At the end of an unending war:
Horizons abide the deception
Of the sky's bright truce

But the dispersals have begun
There are no more roads
Only an immense dew

Of light
Over the dropped leafage
And in the room where

On the music-stand
The silent sonata lies
Open

POEM

space
window
that looks into itself

a facing
both and
every way

colon
between green apple:
and vase of green

invisible
bed and breath
ebb and air-flow

below an unflawed
iridescence
of spiderweb

APPEARANCE

Snow brings into view the far hills:
    The winter sun feels for their surfaces:
Of the little we know of them, full half
    Is in the rushing out to greet them, the restraint
(Unfelt till then) melted at the look
    That gathers them in, to a meeting of expectations
With appearances. And what appears
    Where the slant-sided lit arena opens
Plane above plane, comes as neither
    Question nor reply, but a glance
Of fire, sizing our ignorance up,
    As the image seizes on us, and we grasp
For the ground that it delineates in a flight
    Of distances, suddenly stilled: the cold
Hills drawing us to a reciprocation,
    Ask words of us, answering images
To their range, their heights, held
    By the sun and the snow, between pause and change.

IV. BAGATELLES

ARS POETICA

In memoriam A.A.

WHAT is it for
this form of saying, truce
with history in a language
no one may wish to use?

Who was it said
'a form of suicide'?—meaning
you drive yourself up to the edge
or as near as you can ride

without dropping over.
Some drop, wit-
less—and we
are to praise them for it?

Well, if mourning
were all we had,
we could settle for a great simplicity,
mourn ourselves mad.

But that is only half
the question: blight
has its cures and hopes
come uninvited.

What is it for? Answers
should be prepaid. And no Declines
of the West Full Stop
No selling lines.

MÉLISANDE

FOR Mélisande
flower-child of the forest
there were certain lacunae
in the short history of
her life: stoned
so many times
she could not recall
and she kept losing things
rings and things:
there was so little of her
she was mostly hair
and an impregnable innocence
gave an unthinking
rightness to whatever
she did or did not
do: the men she knew
slipped away
almost unnoticed
(she was not tenacious)
like rings and things:
—I had, she said
when she ended up
'beginning all over again'
and went home—I had
what you might call
a vision: and she needed one:
her mother
had forgotten to tell her
things and there was
nothing at all
half-way in her life such as
sorry or thankyou . . .
but they were together now
and in the evenings
mother sat
and read to her
The Greening of America
and other books like that
and so they lived
vapidly ever after

DIALECTIC

for Edoardo Sanguineti

LIFE is the story of a body, you say:
the cough in the concert-hall is the story
of a body that cannot contain itself,
and the Waldstein the story of a life
refusing to be contained
by its body, the damaged ear
rebegetting its wholeness in posterities
of notes. I uncramp
bent knees. Side by side
all these itching legs! straining
to give back to the body
the rhythm out of the air and
heel-tap it into the ground.
A dropped programme tells
of a body lost to itself
and become all ear—ear
such as only the deaf
could dream of, with its gigantic
channels and circuits, its
snailshell of cartilage
brimming and quivering with the auricle's
passed-on story where
life is the breaking of silences
now heard, the daily remaking a body
refleshed of air.

THE NIGHT-TRAIN

composed
solely of carbon and soot-roses
freighted tight
with a million
minuscule statuettes
of La Notte (Night)

37

stumbles on
between unlit halts
till daylight begins
to bleed its jet
windows white, and the night-
train softly
discomposes, rose
on soot-rose,
to become—white
white white—
the snow-plough
that refuses to go.

EVENT

NOTHING is happening
Nothing

A waterdrop
Soundlessly shatters
A gossamer gives

Against this unused space
A bird
Might thoughtlessly try its voice
But no bird does

On the trodden ground
Footsteps
Are themselves more pulse than sound

At the return
A little drunk
On air

Aware that
Nothing
Is happening

COMEDY

It was when he began to see fields
As arguments, the ribbed ploughland
Contending with the direction of its fence:
If you went with the furrows, the view
From the fence disputed with you
Because you couldn't see it. If you sat still
The horizontals plainly said
You ought to be walking, and when you did
All you were leaving behind you proved
That you were missing the point. And the innumerable views
Kept troubling him, until
He granted them. Amen.

THREE WAGNERIAN LYRICS

1. LIEBESTOD

Tannhäuser wandered in the Venusberg:
    Spring's goddess had him for a season,
And no love living ever gave
    All that he knew there, and still craved
At his return. What could his lady
    Do but die?—She drew him after her
Deeper than ever spring could stir him.

II. THE POTION

King Mark who
Unwilling prognosticator
Of the *grand guignol viennois*
Despaired of ruling
His libidinal relatives,
Apologized
To them for them: 'The potion!
It was not your fault.'

Children of the times,
Absolved, they did not hear
The excuses he came to bring,
For one was dead and the other kept on singing.

III. GOOD FRIDAY

EASTER and the resurrection
  Of the grass. Humbled Kundry
Dries the anointed feet of Parsifal
  With her hair. It is the imprisoned blood
Of Venus glows in the grail cup.

V. INSTEAD OF AN ENDING

OVER ELIZABETH BRIDGE: a circumvention

to a friend in Budapest

. . . my heart which owes this past a calm future.
                                        Attila József, *By the Danube*

THREE years, now, the curve of Elizabeth Bridge
Has caught at some half-answering turn of mind—
Not recollection, but uncertainty
Why memory should need so long to find
A place and peace for it: that uncertainty
And restless counterpointing of a verse
'So wary of its I', Iván, is me:

Why should I hesitate to fix a meaning?
The facts were plain. A church, a riverside,
And, launched at the further bank, a parapet
Which, at its setting-out, must swerve or ride
Sheer down the bulk of the defenceless nave,
But with a curious sort of courteousness,
Bends by and on again. That movement gave

A pause to thoughts, which overeagerly
Had fed on fresh experience and the sense
That too much happened in too short a time
In this one city: self-enravelled, dense
With its own past, even its silence was
Rife with explanations, drummed insistent
As traffic at this church's window-glass.

How does the volley sound in that man's ears
Whom history did not swerve from, but elected
To face the squad? Was it indifference,
Fear, or sudden, helpless peace reflected
In the flash, for Imre Nagy?—another kind
Of silence, merely, that let in the dark
Which closed on Rajk's already silenced mind?

Here, past is half a ruin, half a dream—
Islanded patience, work of quiet hands,
Repainting spandrels that out-arched the Turk
In this interior. These are the lands

Europe and Asia, challenging to yield
A crop, or having raised one, harvest it,
Used for a highroad and a battlefield.

The bridge has paid the past its compliment:
The far bank's statuary stand beckoning
Where it flows, in one undeviating span,
Across the frozen river. That reckoning
Which József owed was cancelled in his blood,
And yet his promise veered beyond the act,
His verse grown calm with all it had withstood.

IN MEMORIAM THOMAS HARDY

How to speak with the dead
so that not only
our but their
words are valid?

Unlike their stones,
they scarcely resist us,
memory adjusting
its shades, its mist:

they are too like their photographs
where we can fill
with echoes of our regrets
brown worlds of stillness.

His besetting word
was 'afterwards' and it released
their qualities, their restlessness
as though they heard it.

REMEMBERING WILLIAMS

'WISH we could talk today'
you wrote—no more
than that: the time before
it was: 'I stumbled
on a poem you had written', but the theme
lost itself, you forgot to say
what it was
'that called to mind
something over which
we had both been working, but had not
worked out by half.' Your wife
said she had done her mourning
while you still lived. Life
is a hard bed to lie on dying.

THE APPARITION

I DREAMED, Justine, we chanced on one another
　　As though it were twenty years ago. Your dark
Too vulnerable beauty shone
　　As then, translucent with its youth,
Unreal, as dreams so often are,
　　With too much life. 'Tomorrow',
You said, 'we plough up the pastureland.'
　　The clear and threatening sky
New England has in autumn—its heightened blue,
　　The promise of early snow—were proofs enough
Of the necessity, though of what pastureland
　　You spoke, I'd no idea. Then
Reading the meaning in your face, I found
　　Your pastureland had been your hallowed ground which now
Must yield to use. And all of my refusals,
　　All I feared, stood countered
By the resolve I saw in you and heard:
　　While death itself, its certain thread
Twisted through the skein of consequence
　　Seemed threatened by the strength

Of those dead years. It was a dream—
    No more; and you whom death
And solitude have tried, must know
    The treachery of dreams. And yet I do not think it lied,
Because it came, without insistence,
    Stood for a moment, spoke and then
Was gone, that apparition,
    Beyond the irresolute confines of the night,
Leaving me to weigh its words alone.

JULIET'S GARDEN

*J'ai connu une petite fille qui quittait son jardin bruyamment, puis
s'en revenait à pas de loup pour 'voir comment il était quand elle n'était
pas là.'*—Sartre

SILENTLY . . .
she was quieter than breathing now,
hearing the garden seethe
behind her departed echo:

flowers merely grew,
showing no knowledge of her:
stones hunching their hardnesses
against her not being there:

scents came penetratingly,
rose, apple, and leaf-rot,
earthsmell under them all,
to where she was not:

such presences could only
rouse her fears,
ignoring and perfuming
this voluntary death of hers:

and so she came rushing back
into her garden then,
her new-found lack
the measure of all Eden.

46

AGAINST PORTRAITS

How, beyond all foresight
or intention, light
plays with a face
whose features play with light:

frame on gilded frame,
ancestor on ancestor,
the gallery is filled
with more certainty than we can bear:

if there must be
an art of portraiture,
let it show us ourselves as we
break from the image of what we are:

the animation of speech, and then
the eyes eluding
that which, once spoken,
seems too specific, too concluding:

or, entering a sudden slant
of brightness, between dark and gold,
a face half-hesitant,
face at a threshold:

GREEN QUINCES

RIPENING there
among the entanglement of leaves
that share their colour—
green quinces:
fragrantly free
from the contaminations
of daily envy,
the sight and suddenness
of green unknot

all that which thought
has ravelled where it cannot span
between the private and the public man—
between the motive
and the word:
the repeated and absurd
impulse to justify
oneself, knows
now its own
true colours:
it was the hardest-to-be-
put-down
vanity—desire
for the regard
of others. And how wrong
they were who taught us
green was the colour
should belong
to envy: they envied green.

DURING RAIN

BETWEEN
slats of the garden
bench, and strung
to their undersides
ride clinging
rain-drops, white
with transmitted
light as the bench
with paint: ranged
irregularly
seven staves of them
shine out
against the space
behind: untroubled
by the least breeze they
seem not to move
but one
by one as if

suddenly ripening
tug themselves free
and splash
down to be
replaced by an identical
and instant twin:
the longer you
look at it
the stillness proves
one flow unbroken
of new, false pearls,
dropped seeds of now
becoming then.

ELEGY FOR HENRY STREET

for George and Mary Oppen

AFTER the flight, the tired body
  Clung to the fading day of Henry Street:
There, it was hardly at an end, but midnight
  Weighed on the pulse of thought, its deep
Inconsistency working behind the eye
  That watched the lights come on—lights
Of the further shore, Manhattan's million
  Windows, floor on floor repeated
By the bay. I liked the street for its sordid
  Fiction of a small town order,
For its less and dingier glass
  As it let one down and back
Slowly out of transatlantic into human time,
  And its sooted bricks declared they were there
As they no longer are. 'Duck!' you cried, George,
  The day the militia filed out with rifles
At a Shriner celebration, but that was the pastoral era
  Of sixty-six, and how should we or they
Have known, as taps were blowing, and the echoes,
  Trapped in each scarred hallway
Meanly rhymed memory with civility,
  They were bugling the burial of a place and time?

MISTLINES

WATCHING the mistlines flow slowly in
  And fill the land's declivities that lay
Unseen until that indistinctness
  Had acknowledged them, the eye
Grasps, at a glance, the mind's own
  Food and substance, shape after shape
Emerging where all shapes drown;
  For the mind is a hunter of forms:
Finding them wherever it may—in firm
  Things or in frail, in vanishings—
It binds itself, in a world that must decay,
  To present substance, and the words
Once said, present and substance
  Both belie the saying. Mist
Drives on the house till forms become
  The shapes of nearness, densities of home
Charged by their solitude—an island of
  Daily objects mist has clarified
To the transparent calm in which you wear
  The vestment of space that separates four walls,
Your flesh as certain and transitory as the world you share.

MOVEMENTS

I.

I WANT that height and prospect such as music
  Brings one to—music or memory,
When memory gains ground drowned-out
  By years. I want the voyage of recovery,
The wind-torn eyrie and the mast-top
  Sight of the horizon island,
Look-out tower compounded from pure sound:
  Trough on trough, valley after valley
Opens across the waves, between the dancing
  Leaves of the tree of time, and the broken chords
Space a footing for melody, borne-out above
  The haven of its still begetting, the hill

Of its sudden capture, not disembodied
    But an incarnation heard, a bird-flight
Shared, thrust and tendon and the answering air.

II.

The sky goes white. There is no bright alternation now
    Of lit cloud on blue: the scene's finality
Is robbed of a resonance. The day will end
    In its misting-over, its blending of muffled tones,
In a looking to nearnesses. A time
    Of colourlessness prepares for a recomposing,
As the prelude of quiet grows towards the true
    Prelude in the body of the hall. Anew we see
Nature as body and as building
    To be filled, if not with sound, then with
The thousand straying filamented ways
    We travel it by, from the inch before us to the height
Above, and back again. For travelling, we come
    To where we were; as if, in the rhymes
And repetitions and the flights of seeing,
    What we sought for was the unspoken
Familiar dialect of habitation—speech
    Behind speech, language that teaches itself
Under the touch and sight: a text
    That we must write, restore, complete
Grasping for more than the bare facts warranted
    By giving tongue to them. The sound
Of the thick rain chains us in liberty to where we are.

III.

Man, in an interior, sits down
    Before an audience of none, to improvise:
He is biding his time, for the rhymes
    That will arise at the threshold of his mind—
Pass-words into the castle-keep,
    The city of sleepers. Wakened by him,
Stanza by stanza (room by room)
    They will take him deeper in. Door
Opens on door, rhyme on rhyme,
    And the circling stair is always nearer
The further it goes. At last,

He will hear by heart the music that he feared
Was lost, the crossing and the interlacing,
    The involutions of its tracery and the answering of part
By part, as the melody recedes, proceeds
    Above the beat, to twine, untwine
In search of a consonance between
    The pulse of the exploration and the pulse of line.

IV.

How soon, in the going down, will he
    Outdistance himself, lose touch to gain
The confidence of what would use him? Where
    Does he stand—beyond the customary ritual,
The habitual prayer? We live
    In an invisible church, a derisible hurt,
A look-out tower, point of powerlessness:
    The kingdom he has entered is a place
Of sources not of silences; memory does not rule it,
    But memory knows her own there
In finding names for them, reading
    By the flames the found words kindle
Their unburnable identities: the going down
    Is to a city of shapes, not a pit of shades
(For all ways begin, either from the eyes out
    Or the eyes in): to a Piazza del Campo
For spirits blessed by a consequence of days;
    For all that would speak itself aloud, a season
Of just regard, a light of sweetened reason.

V.

Man, in an exterior, sits down to say
    What it is he sees before him: to say
Is to see again by the light of speech
    Speechless, the red fox going
With intent, blind-eyed to all
    But prey. Human, our eyes
Stay with the green of an environment
    He only moves through, and man
In an exterior, tutelary spirit
    Of his own inheritance, speaks
To celebrate, entering on this action

That is a sort of acting, this assumption
Of a part where speech must follow
    As natural to the occasion, a doing which
Acts out the doer's being,
    Going beyond itself to clarify
The thing it is. But an actor
    May rehearse, sewing the speech behind his thoughts,
Readying them to come into his mind
    Before the words. Yet here, to think
Is say is see: and the red fox
    Caught where it patrols its cruel Eden,
Sets at a counter-pause
    The track of thought, as mounting the unsteady
Wall of crumbled ragstone, it halts its progress,
    A clear momentary silhouette, before it
Dips and disappears into wordlessness.

VI. WRITTEN ON WATER

One returns to it, as though it were a thread
    Through the labyrinth of appearances, following-out
By eye, the stream in its unravelling,
    Deep in the mud-flanked gash the years
Have cut into scarpland: hard to read
    The life lines of erratic water
Where, at a confluence of two ways
    Refusing to be one without resistance,
Shoulderings of foam collide, unskein
    The moving calligraphy before
It joins again, climbing forward
    Across obstructions: but do you recall
That still pool—it also fed its stream—
    That we were led, night by night,
To return to, as though to clarify ourselves
    Against its depth, its silence? We lived
In a visible church, where everything
    Seemed to be at pause, yet nothing was:
The surface puckered and drew away
    Over the central depth; the foliage
Kept up its liquid friction
    Of small sounds, their multiplicity
A speech behind speech, continuing revelation
    Of itself, never to be revealed:

It rendered new (time within time)
   An unending present, travelling through
All that we were to see and know:
   'Written on water', one might say
Of each day's flux and lapse,
   But to speak of water is to entertain the image
Of its seamless momentum once again,
   To hear in its wash and grip on stone
A music of constancy behind
   The wide promiscuity of acquaintanceship,
Links of water chiming on one another,
   Water-ways permeating the rock of time.

CURTAIN CALL

The dead in their dressing rooms
sweat out the sequel
through greasepaint and brocade
O to have died
on the last note of a motif, flangeing home
the dovetails of sweet necessity. . . . But the applause
draws them on to resurrection.
No one has won.
Time has undone the incurables
by curing them. The searoar of hands
throbbing, ebbing, each castaway
starts to explore his island. Vans
are standing outside now,
ready for palaces and caverns where
past hoardings and houses
boarded against demolition
a late-night traffic
turning its headlamps towards the peripheries gives
caller and called
back to their own unplotted lives.